Who Pushed Humpty?

A Nursery Rhyme Crime
by H. O. O. Dunnit
(Alias Dianne Bates and Mary Small)
Illustrated by Craig Smith

There is a rhyme we all recall,
that tells of Humpty and his fall.

From the wall he fell headlong —
but how did it happen? What went wrong?

Was Humpty pushed? Was it a crime?
We'll look at the suspects, one at a time.

First the old woman, who lived in a shoe:
she had lots of children — all hungry, too.

Did she see Humpty, high on the wall, and plan an omelette to feed them all?

Did she push Humpty?

Up the hill went Jill with Jack,
up to the well at the top of the track.

Jack fell down and broke his crown —
did Jill push Jack *and* Humpty down?

Did she push Humpty?

The Duke of York marched all his men to the top of the hill and down again.

And what did that army think of most?
Was it Humpty, served on toast?

Did they push Humpty?

There was a little girl, who had a little curl, who could be good — or horrid.

In a bad temper, late one night,
did she push Humpty, out of spite?

Did she push Humpty?

In the dark, Tom Tom ran by,
with a squealing pig from a farmer's sty.

"Stop thief!" cried Humpty from the wall.
"Be quiet," hissed Tom, "or you might fall."

Did he push Humpty?

Or maybe, while alone one night,
Humpty saw the strangest sight.

A cow was jumping over the moon;
a dish was running away with a spoon!

Did Humpty laugh and wobble around?
Could this be how he fell to the ground?

Maybe no one pushed Humpty!

But someone else we shouldn't neglect
is little Jack Horner, a prime suspect.

After pie — all sugar and spice —
a simple egg might be quite nice.

Did he push Humpty?

And little Bo Peep, when she lost her sheep, might have grown tired of looking.

Did she see Humpty on the wall —
and begin to think of cooking?

Did she push Humpty?

The suspects now have all been named.

Look at them closely. Who's to blame?

Who Knows?

Treasure Hunting
Huberta the Hiking Hippo
The Present from Aunt Skidoo
Alfie's Gift
The Very Thin Cat of Alloway Road
Hunting with My Camera

The Droughtmaker
Crocodilians
Who Pushed Humpty?
The Golden Goose
Trains
The Ballad of Robin Hood

Written by **H.O.O. Dunnit** (alias Mary Small and Dianne Bates)
Illustrated by **Craig Smith**
Designed by **Christine Deering**

Previously published in *Literacy 2000*.

© Illustrations 1999 Mimosa Publications Pty Limited
All rights reserved

05 04 03 02 01 00 99
10 9 8 7 6 5 4 3 2 1

Published by Mimosa Publications Pty Limited,
P.O. Box 779, Hawthorn, Victoria 3122, Australia

Distributed in the United States of America by

a division of Reed Elsevier Inc.
500 Coventry Lane
Crystal Lake, IL 60014
800-822-8661

Printed through Bookbuilders Limited, Hong Kong
ISBN 0 7327 2494 5

Rigby
ISBN: 0-7327-2494-5